Daphnis et Chloé
Suite No. 2

Maurice Ravel

DOVER PUBLICATIONS, INC.
Mineola, New York

Bibliographical Note

This Dover edition, first published in 1999, is an unabridged republication of *Daphnis & Chloé / Ballet en un Acte / Fragments Symphoniques / 2ᵉ Série: Lever du jour—Pantomime—Danse générale,* originally published by Editions Durand & Cⁱᵉ, Paris, 1913.

Lists of contents, credits and instrumentation, as well as a program and glossary are newly added. English translations by Ronald Herder were specially prepared for this edition.

International Standard Book Number: 0–486–40640-7

Manufactured in the United States of America
Dover Publications, Inc., 31 East 2nd Street, Mineola, N.Y. 11501

CONTENTS

Note: Ravel drew six tableaux of "symphonic fragments" from his original ballet score, dividing them equally between two orchestral suites ("séries"). Rehearsal numbers in these scores run consecutively, accounting for the appearance of late rehearsal number 155 on page 1 of the present edition.

1

I. Lever du jour *(Daybreak)*

40

II. Pantomime

75

III. Danse générale

DAPHNIS ET CHLOÉ

Ballet in one act

In the form of a pastoral romance
attributed to the Greek author Longus (3rd c. B.C.).
Composed 1902–12 for Serge Diaghilev's Ballets Russes,
and first performed on 8 June 1912 at the Théâtre du Châtelet, Paris.

Music by Maurice Ravel

CREDITS FOR THE ORIGINAL PRODUCTION

Choreography. . . . . Michel Fokine
Decor and costumes . . . . Léon Bakst
Musical direction . . . . Pierre Monteux

Daphnis . . . . Vaslav Nijinsky
Chloé. . . . . Thamara Karsavina

The great god Pan. Pirates, led by Bryaxis.
Dorcon and Lyceion. The old shepherd Lammon.
Shepherds and shepherdesses. Nymphs and satyrs.

THE ORCHESTRAL SUITES

While working on the ballet, Ravel extracted two orchestral suites from the score, subtitled "Fragments Symphoniques." Suite No. 1 consists of the three tableaux *Nocturne, Interlude* and *Danse guerrière* (Warrior's dance). Suite No. 2 consists of *Lever du jour* (Daybreak), *Pantomime* and *Danse générale*.

PROGRAM

[Score page 1]: There is no noise other than the murmur of the tiny streams fed by the dew that drips from the rocks. [2]: Daphnis reclines as always before the nymphs' grotto. [4-5]: *DAYBREAK:* Dawn comes little by little . . . We hear birdsongs. [13]: A shepherd passes at a distance with his flock. [16]: Another shepherd crosses downstage. [23-4]: A group of shepherds enter, seeking Daphnis and Chloé. [25-6]: They find Daphnis and awaken him . . . Alarmed, he looks around for Chloé. [27-8]: At last she appears, surrounded by shepherdesses . . . The reunited lovers embrace fervently. [30-1]: Daphnis notices the wreath of flowers encircling Chloe's brow. His dream was a prophetic vision: Pan's intervention is obvious. [In the tableau preceding "Daybreak," Chloé had been abducted by pirates, then rescued by Pan as the pirates fled in disarray.]

[Score page 39]: The old shepherd Lammon explains that Pan saved Chloé in remembrance of the nymph Syrinx whom he once loved. [40-1]: *PANTOMIME:* Daphnis and Chloé mime the story of Pan and Syrinx . . . Chloé portrays the young nymph wandering in the meadow. [42-3]: Daphnis appears as Pan, declaring his love . . . The nymph turns away from him. The god becomes more insistent. [44]: She disappears in the reeds of the meadow. In despair, Pan gathers several stalks, shaping a flute on which he plays a melancholy air. [45]: Chloé reappears and dances to his music, reflecting in her movements the accents of the flute. [59-60]: The dance gradually becomes livelier and, in a dizzying whirl, Chloé falls into the arms of Daphnis. [67-8]: Before the nymphs' altar, Daphnis swears his faith on two ewes . . . A group of young girls enter, dressed as bacchantes, shaking tambourines. [70-1]: Daphnis and Chloé embrace tenderly. A group of young men break onto the scene . . . Joyous commotion. [75]: *GENERAL DANCE.* [87]: Daphnis and Chloé. [91]: Dorcon.

End of the ballet.

ix

INSTRUMENTATION

Piccolo [Petite Flûte, P^te Fl.]
2 Flutes [Grandes Flûtes, G^des Fl.]
Flute in G [Fl(ûte) en Sol]
2 Oboes [Hautbois, Htb.]
English Horn [Cor Anglais, Cor A.]
E♭ Clarinet [Petite Clarinette en Mi♭ , P^te Cl.]
2 Clarinets in A, B♭ [Clarinettes en La, Si♭ , Cl.]
Bass Clarinet in B♭ [Clarinette Basses en Si♭ , Cl. B.]
3 Bassoons [Bassons, B^ons]
Contrabassoon [Contrebasson, C. B^on]

4 Horns in F [Cors en Fa]
4 Trumpets in C [Trompettes en Ut, Trp.]
3 Trombones [Trombones, Trb.]
Tuba

Timpani [Timbales, Timb.]

Percussion *(in score order)*
    Triangle [Tri(angle), Trg.]
    Cymbals [Cymbales, Cymb.]
    Bass Drum [Grosse-Caisse, Gr. Caisse, G.C.]
    Field Drum [Tambour, Tamb.]
    Snare Drum [Caisse Claire, C^sse Cl., C. Cl.]
    Castanets [Castagnettes, Cast.]
    Tambourine [Tambour Basque, T. de B.]
    Glockenspiel [Jeu de Timbres, J. de T.]

Celesta [Célesta, Cél.]
2 Harps [Harpes, Hrp.]

Full *(wordless)* Chorus [Sop., Contr., Tén., Bas.]
    Orchestral parts contain Ravel's instrumental
    alternatives to the choral lines.

Violins 1, 2 [Violons, V^ons]
Violas [Altos, Alt.]
Cellos [Violoncelles, V^elles]
Basses [Contrebasses, C.B.] *(with low C string)*

xi

GLOSSARY

animé, lively
animez un peu, become a little livelier
au (1ᵉʳ) mouvement (mouvᵗ) = Tempo I, a tempo
avec mailloche, with a large mallet [percussion]
avec un peu plus de la langueur, with a bit more languor

bag(uette) d'éponge, sponge-tipped percussion beater

cédez (très peu), hold back (a little)
corde, string

derrière la scène, offstage

en animant toujours (davantage), becoming constantly livelier (still)
en dehors, to the fore, bring out
en s'éloignant, withdrawing
en 3, en 4 = a3, a4
et, and
étouffez, damp [the harp strings]
express(if) (et souple), expressive (and yielding)

jeu ord(inaire), play in the usual way [cancels previous instruction]
jusqu'à, until

lent, slow

moins animé, less lively

Otez les sourdines une à une en commençant par les chefs de pupitres,
Toute doivent être enlevées à 156. [Footnote, p. 1]

    Remove the mutes one by one beginning with the principals at
    each desk. Removal must be completed by 156.

plus, more
plus lent, slower
plus près, closer
précédente, preceding
prenez, take [exchange one instrument for another]
pressez (le 2d temps), rush ahead (the second time)

retenez (peu à peu) = *ritenuto (poco a poco)*
retenu (légèrement), held back (lightly)

sans sourdines, unmuted, *senza sordini*
sourd(ines), mutes
suivez le solo, follow the solo
sur la scène, onstage
sur la touche, on the fingerboard, *sul tasto*
sur le sol (ré, ut, etc.*),* on the G (D, C, etc.) string

toujours = *sempre*
très = *molto*
très court, very short
très ralenti = *molto ritardando*

un peu plus animé, a little livelier

vif, brisk, animated

Daphnis et Chloé
Suite No. 2

Daphnis est toujours étendu devant la grotte des Nymphes.

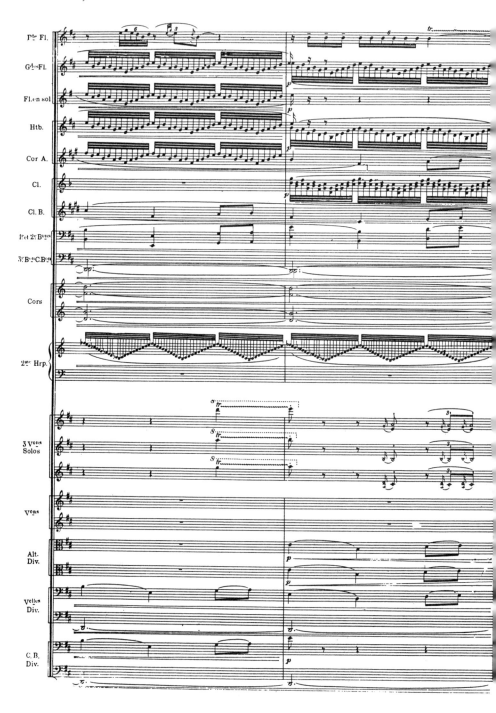

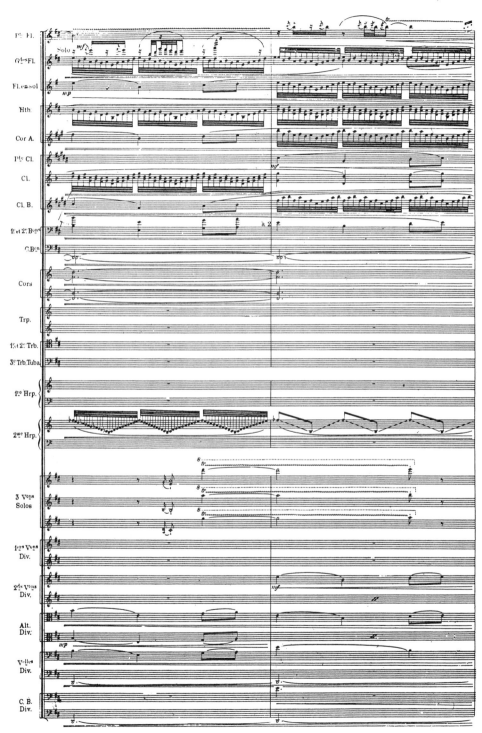

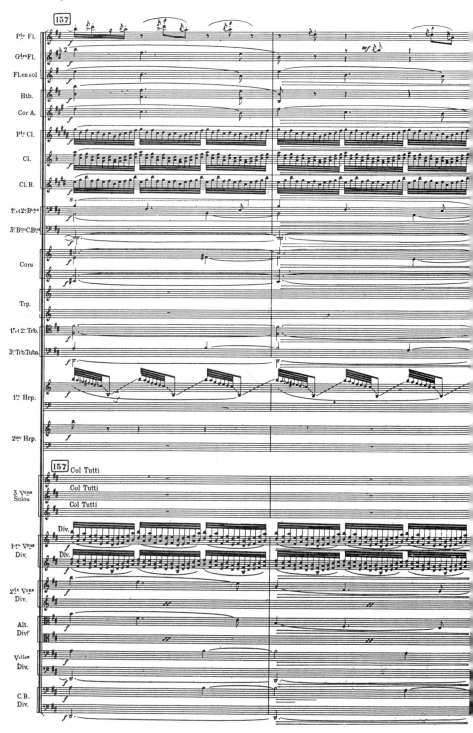

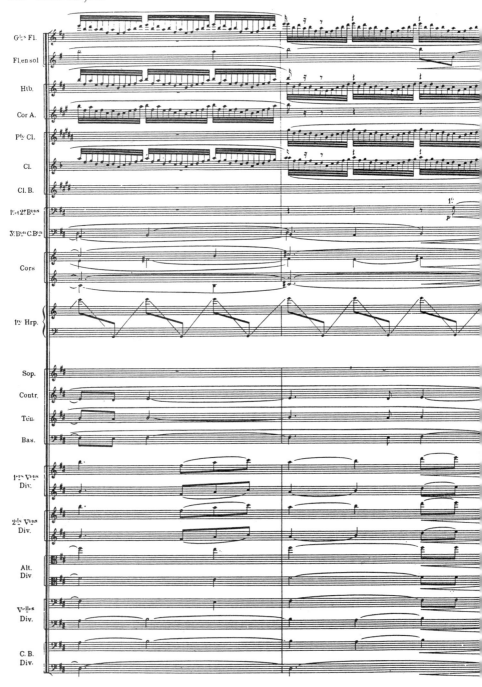

Entre un groupe de pâtres à la recher-

Ils découvrent Daphnis et le réveillent

Elle apparaît enfin, entourée de bergères.

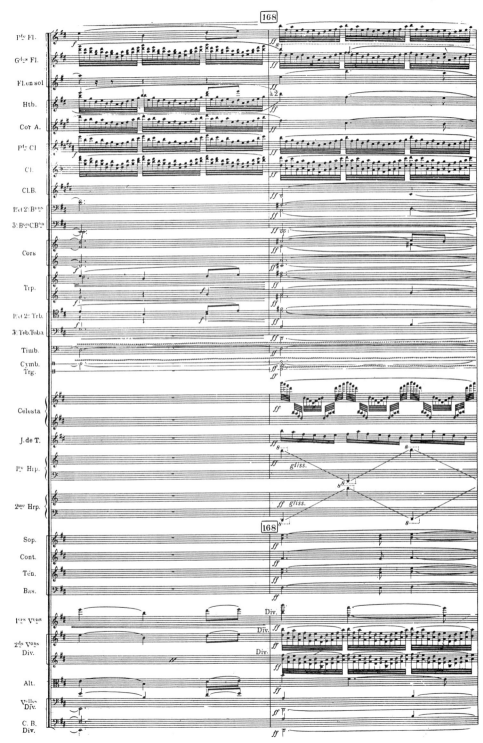

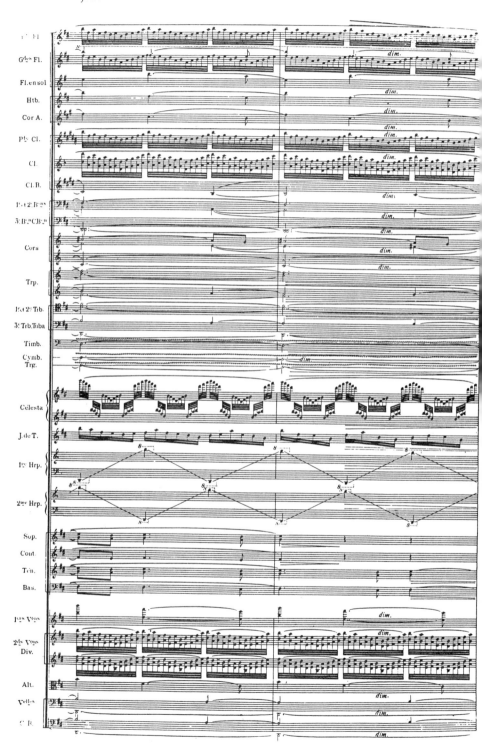

Le vieux berger Lammon explique que, si Pan a sauvé Chloé, c'est en souvenir de la nymphe Syrinx, dont le dieu fut épris

Chloé figure la jeune nymphe errant dans la prairie.

Elle disparaît dans les roseaux. Désespéré, il arrache quelques tiges en forme une flûte et joue un air mélancolique.

178 au Mouvt
Retenu
Fl.
Htb.
Cor A.
Cl.
Cors
Hrp.
Hrp.
178 au Mouvt
Retenu
arco
pizz
Unis pizz.
arco
Unis
Alt.
Div.
arco
Div.

Pte Fl.
Gdes Fl.
Fl. en sol
Htb.
Cor A.
Cl.
Bons
Cors
Cél.
1re Hrp.
pizz. Unis
1ers Vons Div.
pizz. Unis
Unis
2ds Vons Div.
Unis
Alt. Div.
Velles Div.
C. B. Div.

183 En animant toujours davantage
Pte Fl.
Gdes Fl.
Fl. en sol
Htb.
Cor A.
Cl.
Cl. B.
Bon
Cors
Trg.
Cymb.
Tamb.
T. de B.
1re Hrp.
2me Hrp.
183 En animant toujours davantage
1ers Vons Div.
2ds Vons Div.
Alt. Div.
Vclles Div.
C. B.

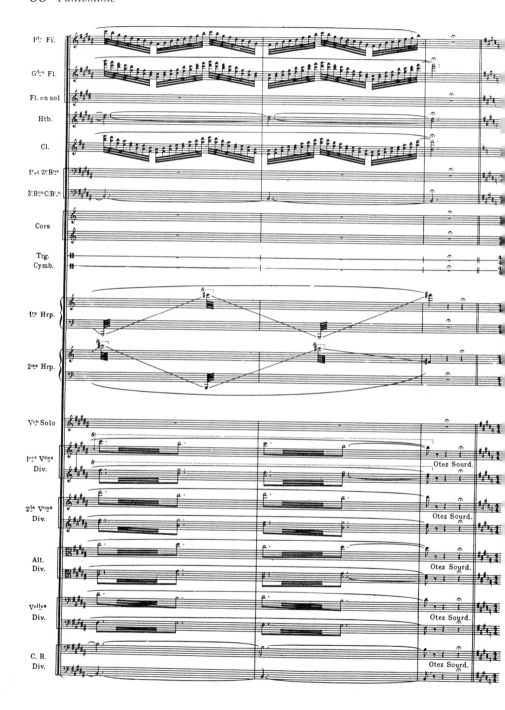

Devant l'autel des Nymphes, il jure sa foi, sur deux brebis.

Entre un groupe de jeunes filles costumées en bacchantes, agitant des tambourins.

Fl.
Fl.
en sol
Htb.
Cor A.
Cl.
Cl.
C.Bon
Cors
Trp.
2e Trb.
Tuba
Trg.
Cymb.
Tamb.
Cast.
de B.
Hrp.
Hrp.
gliss.
Vons Div.
Vons Div.
Alt. Div.
Celles Div.
C. B. Div.
ff
f

Daphnis et Chloé s'enlacent tendrement. Un groupe de jeunes hommes envahit la scène.

198
Pte Fl.
Gdes Fl.
Fl. en sol
Htb.
Cor A.
Pte Cl.
Cl.
Cl. B.
1r et 2e Bons
3e Bon C.Bon
Cors
Trp.
1r et 2e Trb.
3e Trb. Tuba
Trg.
G. C.
Cymb.
Tamb.
C. Cl.
T. de B.
1re Hrp.
2me Hrp.
198
1ers Vons Div.
2ds Vons Div.
Alt. Div.
Velles Div.
C. B. Div.

199
Fl.
Htb.
Cor A.
Cl.
Cl.B.
Cors
Sourdines
2e ôtez la Sourdine
ôtez les Sourdines
Trp.
Timb.
Hrp.
Danse générale
199
pizz.
Alt.
Div.
C. B.
Div.

Pts Fl.
Gdes Fl.
Fl. en sol
Htb.
Cor A.
Pte Cl.
Cl.
Cl. B.
1r et 2e Bons
3e Bon C. Bon
Cors
Trp.
1r et 2e Trb.
3e Trb. Tuba
Timb.
Trg.
Cymb.
G. C.
Tamb.
Cnes Cl.
Cast.
T. de B.
1re Hrp.
2me Hrp.
1ers Vons Div.
2ds Vons Div.
Alt. Div.
Vcelles Div.
C. B. Div.
à 2
pizz
arco
en 2
en 3

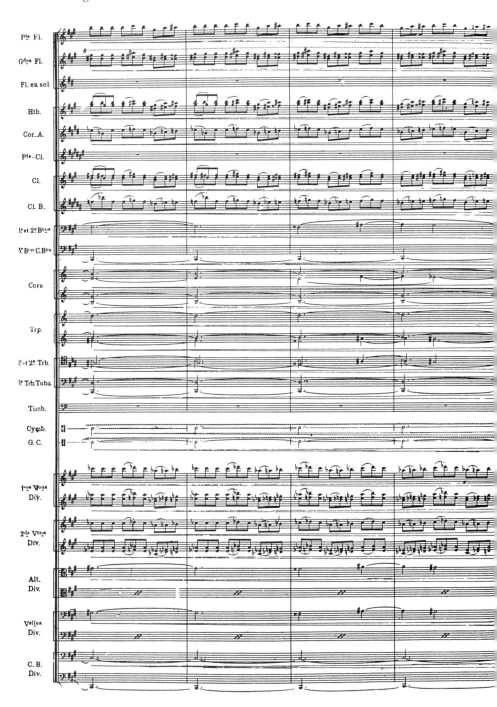

Fl.
Fl.
en sol
Htb.
Cor A.
Cl.
Cl.
Cl. B.
2e Bons
C.Bon
Cors
Trp.
2e Trb.
Trb. Tuba
Timb.
Cymb.
G. C.
Vons
Div.
Vons
Div.
Alt.
Div.
Div.
C. B.
Div.

Gde Fl.
Htb.
Cor A.
Pte Cl.
Cl.
Cl. B.
1er et 2e Bons
Cors
Trp.
Trb.
Trg.
Cymb.
Tamb.
Csse Cl.
Cast.
T. de B.
1re Hrp.
Sop.
Contr.
Tén.
Bas.
1ers Vons
Div.
2ds Vons
Div.
pizz.
arco
en 2
en 3
Alt.
Div.
Vlles
Div.
C. B.
Div.

1re Fl.
Gde Fl.
Fl. en sol
Htb.
Cor A.
1re Cl.
Cl.
Cl. B.
1re et 2e Bons
Cors
Trp.
Trb.
Trg.
Cymb.
Tamb.
Cse Cl.
Cast.
T. de B.
1re Hrp.
Mi♭ Sol♭ Si♮
Sop.
Contr.
Tén.
Bas.
1ers Vons Div.
2ds Vons Div.
pizz.
arco
Alt. Div.
Velles Div.
C. B. Div.

Fl.
Fl.
en sol
Htb.
or A.
Cl.
Cl.
B.
2e Bons
C.Bon
Cors
Trp.
2e Trb.
Trb. Tuba
Timb.
Cast.
de B.
Vons
Div.
Vons
Div.
Alt.
Div.
celles
Div.
C. B.
Div.
à 2
1er
3e
1re
arco
f
mf
p
mp
pp
tr

Fl.
Fl
sol
tb.
A.
Cl.
B.
C.Bon
rs
2e Trp
rb.
Hrp.
op.
ntr.
én.
as.
Vons
iv.
lt.
lles
B.
à 2
arco
pizz.
p
f
mf

221
Ptes Fl.
Gdes Fl.
Fl. en sol
Htb.
Cor. A.
Pte Cl.
Cl.
Cl. B.
1r et 2e Bons
3e Bon C.Bon
Cors.
Trp.
1r et 2e Trb.
3e Trb. Tuba
Timb
Trg.
Cymb.
G. C.
Tamb.
Csse Cl.
Cast.
T. de B.
J. de T.
1re Hrp.
2me Hrp.
Sop. Contr.
Tén.
Bas.
221
1ers Vons Div.
gliss.
2ds Vons Div.
gliss.
Alt. Div.
Velles Div.
pizz. arco
C. B. Div.
pizz. arco
pizz. arco
pizz. arco
pizz. arco

END OF EDITION